MOOSEWOOD SANDHILLS

BOOKS BY TIM LILBURN

Names of God (1986)

From the Great Above She Opened
Her Ear to the Great Below (with Susan Shantz) (1988)

Tourist to Ecstasy (1989)

Moosewood Sandhills (1994)

MOOSEWOOD SANDHILLS

poems by

Tim Lilburn

CANADIAN CATALOGUING IN PUBLICATION DATA

Lilburn, Tim, 1950–
Moosewood sandhills

Poems.

ISBN 0-7710-5322-3

I. Title.

PS8573.I52M6 1994 C811'.54 C94-930021-7
PR9199.3.L55M6 1994

Typesetting by M&S

The publishers acknowledge the support of the Canada Council, the Ontario Arts Council, and the Ontario Ministry of Culture, Tourism and Recreation for their publishing program.

Printed and bound in Canada on acid-free paper.

McClelland & Stewart Inc.
The Canadian Publishers
481 University Avenue
Toronto, Ontario
M5G 2E9

1 2 3 4 5 98 97 96 95 94

to Susan

CONTENTS

The words "Moosewood Sandhills" appear only on old maps. They name a large rise of hummocky aspen land on either side of the South Saskatchewan River about a hundred miles south-west of the confluence with the North Saskatchewan. Cactus land, dry scrub, wolf willow, buffalo bean, still place to which the dead are believed to meander, deer and coyote country. I moved in, planted thin gardens, dug a root cellar, slept in the fields under summer stars – and *looked.* How to be in the world as if it were home? Looking with care and desire seemed a political act. The century was closing.

They came to Citeaux, which was then a place of horror, a vast wilderness. Realizing that the asperity of the place accorded well with the strict design they had already conceived, they found the place, almost as if divinely prepared, to be as alluring as their design had been dear.

– *Exordium Cistercii*

IN THE HILLS, WATCHING

Among the nerved grass, thrones,
dominions of grass, in chokecherry dewlapped hills,
hills buffalo-shouldered with shag of pulsed heat, meek hills,
sandhills of rose-hip and aster, in the philanthropic silence
fluxed by the grass, hounded, nervous with its own uncountability, grass
the frail piston of all,
in hill heat, lying down in the nearness of deer.
All knowing darkens as it builds.
The grass is a mirror that clouds as the bright look goes in.
You stay in the night, you squat in the hills in the cave of night. Wait.
Above, luminous rubble, torn webs of radio signals.
Below, stone scrapers, neck bone of a deer, salt beds.
The world is ending.

ACEDIA

You are sitting in the trailer.
Your intellect is with you.
The moon comes into the aspens, closest to earth
                                        in years; almost dawn.
Your senses meet on the blue rug,
                              assembling a passage, prong, into the real,
                                   passing over, boat with the musk of light.
You'd like to be the novice of a deer.
You'd do whatever it told you.

Coyotes flicker by the river.
The moon comes to aspen bush, snow, slope of blond grass.
The river is from badlands,
                         boneland and wind.
You are terrified of having nothing.

CONTEMPLATION IS MOURNING

You lie down in the deer's bed.
It is bright with the undersides of grass revealed by her weight during the
length of her sleep. No one comes here; grass hums
because the body's touched it. Aspen leaves below you sour like horses
after a run. There are snowberries, fescue.
This is the edge of the known world and the beginning of philosophy.

Looking takes you so far on a leash of delight, then removes it and says
the price of admission to further is your name. Either the desert
and winter
of what the deer is in herself or a palace life disturbed by itches and sounds
felt through the gigantic walls. Choose.

Light comes through pale trees as mind sometimes kisses the body.
The hills are the bones of hills.

The deer cannot be known. She is the Atlantic, she is Egypt, she is
the night where her names go missing, to walk into her oddness is
to feel severed, sick, darkened, ashamed.

Her body is a border crossing, a wall and a perfume and past this
she is infinite. And it is terrible to enter this.

You lie down in the deer's bed, in the green martyrion, the place where
language buries itself, waiting place, weem.
You will wait. You will lean into the darkness of her absent
body. You will be shaved and narrowed by the barren strangeness of the
deer, the wastes of her oddness. Snow is coming. Light is cool,
nearly drinkable; from grass protrudes the hard, lost
smell of last year's melted snow.

STABILITY

You go into the shy hills.
You are sorry.
Large winds are falling inside things.
Momentum from Descartes leaning into fire, wax melting in his hand.
Maelstrom of concupiscence dampening in the evening of things.
And against this the world turns too beautiful.
You elope into grass,
into hills' heavy light, into winter pale grass.
Res extensa, reliquary of chaos.
The hills are dark, mid-Atlantic, wilderness made
                                        by no one thinking about it.
Clouded with the jived, ambidextrous eccentricity of the grass.
Lean room for the ear, stone in the sea,
coyote-lit, the hills.
Sit on wind-snapped poplar;
quill-brown hummocks and saucers, grass
                                        a museum of violations of expectation.
First moths shake from snow, history flows
to its lure at the thinnest point
on the mainland of the invented life.
You wait in the cave of the hills.
You have been stared at by deer and
must grow smaller.

REST

Snow falls in the Moosewood Sandhills, on ghost
burrows, deer woods, in the bone-home,
last snow.
What does it mean to become nothing?
You've dug a cave in the earth,
room of knowing, room of tears.
It means to place yourself beneath irrational things
and know they are without blame.
The potato smell of the dark.
You've given up.

Candles of sprouts lengthen, twitching against the wall.
Dry; at seven feet, a galaxy arm
of antelope skeleton; near, stones that give off forehead gleams
of concentration.
Listen to the guttural cable,
drift sand and forest mould,
flaked stone tools
streaming in their motionlessness.
There are fox alone in the hills and grass

far down in the dark tunnel of its strangeness.
Grass enclaustered in the Cistercian vault
of its strangeness. Long night.
All things are vowed to themselves.

FROM AN ANCHORAGE

for J.Z.

*

I've come to the desert.
White grass above snow, coyotes, the heavy stars.
I am looking, I am obedient.
A big weeping's coming.
Something in us, not the banquet or shapely light of consciousness,
not the stone-brothered body, call it the swallowed animal, call
it the cloud or a glowing sleep,
now hears the faint tune of a story in the opulent night around us,
in the forests of our desires and begins to whistle it into the future,
bearing us along with it away from ourselves
floating,
until we come to frozen deer beds on juniper slopes,
the cruxes of the given trees of the aspen bush, beehive huts
of listening on the cliff wall of the century
and linger there while falling in us
against the strain of our hearing which is outward, upward,
clots of darkness are dropping, falling dangerously,
first tears of the necessary apology.
How did we get here, we wonder.

There's a river, too, old, earth-coloured.
The river shrugs from rotting hills, cottonwoods, shimmer of white tail.
Illuminated stupidity, an unknowing you could hold weddings in.
I could go to confession with it, I'd like to loop rosaries
through its long horns.
Bone of water, sleep of the land, from moon flats, cattle trails,
it slouches through the hairy country,
heavy, half-clay, soft-mouthed unremembering of height,
hovel of power, soft-bellied river, blessed cello
of force stroked dark into earth.
Ice on it now as storks the shoulders of the dead.
We don't know how to be here, do we?
We don't know what to give or sacrifice.

*

Desire is loaned to us by the dead.
What are you doing?
I stare at the grass.
Long, white, it is government.
It gleam-shivers like the singing in tongues.
The estuary, the mouth of the woman who is shy, flinched
                from herself, strangers round her, the voice distant, in her,
frightening her with arousal.

I've been here six months.
The stars have changed.
Bones boil up in the mealy earth.
The grader skims them on the pale road.
Their light beats against the house.
They want something from me.

*

Come into this land, this flagellation.
You've been dreaming the great liturgies of reparation.
Your yearning goes ahead of you now as a trail of corn from that
earlier visit.
It's all right, safe. Look, a gold rope into this sleep. Come.

There's nothing here, winter now, hawk country the hawks
abandoned, grouse tracks through snow, the moon close and bright.
The land is bone, dark locks of meat frayed to an end,
the land is badly scraped hide.
Land you should bring something to bury into, old blood, a ring,
bring a scourge, bring a few ideas on the back of an envelope
toward some stiff ordo.
Think of yourself as a child wooed by a wall behind which the adults
are arguing.
A monk.

Now's the weeping time.
Now is when the music must wait for the raw a cappella of apology to rise
shimmering.

Now that voice must rise.
I've found a radar station north of here in snow hills, lost, odd, paint strips
        falling like dirty hair from the aluminum bubble, alone.
Empty yourself, be alone.
Love the earth as felt and grease, love it,
                                heavy bread of leafmould, deer shit and moon light.
Hunker down.
Knowing in the end relaxes into the shining pose of a desire
                        to kneel and scrape the walls of a coyote hole
                            deserted in a sand hill slope into a room to lie in,
                                white roots above you, air scarred with your breath.
Wait for the animals to appear with scrolls in their hooves.
Wait for the gold-tipped deer
                        to come and incense you with the fragrance of their stare.

THINGS RECEDE, EVERYTHING RECEDES, EVERYTHING IS FAR AWAY

Moon in white trees.
Hawks, great horned owls scouting the blank gullies.
In fire-dead bush, fever of the new moon
floats, late afternoon, in faint trees.
Land with a cast, left-handed, cowlicked, the odd
trailer parked among wild roses, someone moved in with his dogs.

Origen says to wait for the amassing of the unions of Paradise.
One world following another as the light in bodies moves
toward the prize.
The way back will be hard, ghost road through the rooms of sorrow,
moon of contemplation on our backs.
It will not feel like virtue, or wonder, or loving things.
Desire will make us walk that gang-plank.

Poplars are gathered into themselves. Fox too. The distance of things,
a lit and horrible separateness.

THE GIFT OF TEARS

You will wait here
in the slow place.
You will wait in a hole. In your forehead, one scar of light,
intimate, thrumming.
The land is thunder laid in a snowy owl's ear,
it shimmers with fossils of fish and palm.

Weed above snow is golden with the absence of a name
and tracks quiver with the spirit-wake of masterfully foreign bodies.
You will try to remember.
At hill root, twenty feet below the sand floor,
tight pools of red water.
You will be true in the pit, you climb
to the capital of the ear's ruined column.

NO ONE REMEMBERS HOW TO DO THIS

Dry snow coming down in the hills.
Magpies hair-triggered and thuggish in worn trees.
A wall has started to fall in you, it will take years to land.
A mule train bearing casks of tears works to the coast
through thick mountains.

You are small and looking.
Deer, their bodies sweating fanned pounds of light, browse
juniper on the north slopes.

No order sings across the flat, there is no order.
These are the songs of the place.
One, The moon rises early and by dawn is in aspen bush.
Another, Deer touch each other with their hooves as they eat.

You were chased here by a darkness.
Listen to the curve of the hills, the guttering voice.
The way to anywhere leads through humiliation.
There are only animal trails.

CONTEMPLATIO

Deer among the chokecherries, in the blue wood, deer.
This is seeing: to be looked at by deer,
to float on the cardiac line hummed into you by the tremoring stare,
to fatten with shadows pennanting from those gusted eyeballs, gathering
to a glistening stop.
Pale paths through aspen, june-grass, pools
of densest dropseed restored into you from beyond.
You don't know who you are.
Go out, walk.
Rose-hips burnt red with frost, wolf willow, sage.
Coyotes have set cairns of hard shit on the paths.
The world sings itself against you.

Thick herds under the flannel earth,
peccary, buffalo, bone-crushing dogs, breathing.
Keep a Siwash over your pajamas till noon, wait.
Something's going to be whispered.
A darkness pulsing up the ten-foot needle grass root from the water table.
And the river, the river strums deep in the bone of the land.

PIETY

Beneath this earth, tensed libraries of tears.
Lectionaries, hermetica, dust, the perfumed inks.
In Cyrillic, wolf.
They could snap the shy clay, they are the hidden lives of the
bright world, the lost turbines.
They have faces of horses terrified by thunder, they drum-roll
in ur-monasteries of clay.
Still codexes, complete archive of amnesia: impacted winds,
a heaving in the tombs.
Animals, they hunch in domes of poplar wattle, with heavy neck muscles.
They will come out with the bone god, the bluestem god, rank with night,
bearing the future.
They will rise, move among us and eroticize everything.
They are the braided song of the end.
But they must not be sung.
Take three or four, stutterers, pale, to sleep three nights
on the earth, the water reaching up to know them.
Let one dream the tears as fruit on the thick wine-soaked tables of the dead
and eat one, its anise flesh, the waxy, lightless pits,
blackout, wake, his forehead touching
a white trunk,
whispering in the name of us all for mercy.

TO THE LEFT OF EVERYTHING

This isn't the Main Event.
You're alive in a white trash doublewide among poplars.
Engine heads in grass, sink parts deeper in trees.
You could hold your beautiful gaze like a hand out to the world, say
"here pup," and it'd come.
To the left of everything, so jacked with feeling your
pectorals hulk like owls, astronaut material for the
Ptolemy Society, a flying boy.
Angels spitfire toward you stroking little Jesuit whips, pieces of cleated
chicken wire to rope hard to your thigh. You, hero of the rod.
Inconsequence or bust. You study for this, crack the books,
ram it to the mat.
At best you could make Doorman
to the bedroom of Hermes Trismegistus.

One afternoon, disgusted, bravo, you fall asleep.
You see yourself in a ballroom, your passions seated before you
in evening dress, swallow tails, bustles, opera glasses, pearls.
You walk to the podium, turn to the orchestra
and conduct the overture to the master opera of neglect.

Purity of heart – wow!
Sounds performing without net erasing into wilderness of air.
Melodious, rambling rottings-away of bright edifices.
Desire gone to the drug store and never seen again.

SOLO ON ORTHODOXY

Two coyotes slouch-jog out of the moth-coloured trees down to the river
after supper, jive-dekes, weightless as Amway sales talk,
a garage sale of moves.
This is the life of light in matter.
This is the flesh.
Tertullian would carve this with a blowtorch.
But me, what do I know; just a Baden-Powell Platonist, jack-Catholic,
slo-pitch cognoscente; I'm nearly a criminal, know diddly and I want
to lay my breath right alongside the way these coyotes move.
I'd be healed, then; I'd be gold,
fanfares shining through flesh.
The river is divine and dumb, doesn't know a thing. Cranes walk
in it, nearly dark; the last hawk caresses over charred aspens near the hill.
Maybe the coyote's shady glide, bluff-lambada, is evangelical,
a note in a tongues of glides and shuffles sung out in trance.
It goes out, say, shows some leg and hooks Lucifer
with its shapes and hover, croons the red bastard into a taste to be it,
raptured hustle, the actual route or flight plan he'll one day
be love-pistoned, sweet-toothed to take (out of the blind
spot, in from the sea, under radar) into the church basement

hall, pulling up a chair at the Holy Martyrs Fowl Supper,
how's it going, talking crops, neighbourly.
"Everything," he'll say then, "will be saved," amazed. Everything,
he'll say, spreading his hands, shrugging.

BIG QUILL LAKE

A steep male emptiness on a salt plain,
silence that burned down from outer space.
Deer, a jackrabbit big as a motorcycle.
You've been sung here by the ledge of the precipice of history,
shrugged from the knife of the will at your throat.
Your mind was music played in another room behind heavy walls. Now
you're here.

Dogwood rise from alkaline crust.
Your derangement is apostolic.
Your ghosts are Saulteaux and Celts.
Lie on this white earth; sleep; the shape your body sighs into the crackling
grass will be a boat bearing you to the interior of the one
rubbing stone the carcass of the lake has rotted from.
Snow geese blurt from the sky, land palpitating on the pale water.
Behind them, the green, grass-odoured spine-valley of the continent.
The lake is dead, blazing with heavy, nervous birds.
On the shore, blue grama grass, buffalo vertebrae. You must wait.

THE COMPUNCTION OF CONSCIOUSNESS

It rides the shoulders of a deer into the high coulees in evening,
into nighthawk-coloured hills,
below breezes passed among planets and stars, after snow-rain,
through poplar islands tingling with the secrecies of water,
through juniper and bearberry and into the pastures of antelope and owl.
Ascesis and return. Intention alive only on the bare rocks
of the wild islands of things.
Cactus alert in its fencing suit.
Red tail closing its wings.
Light loosens from all that is and, at last, bones in blue-grey grass.
Rain-smoke staggers east. Coyote's eyes appear; willow flower's meek
in its scent.
Deer take bleary paths into the palisades as one breath follows another.
The ego rests on the pillow of their dexterity.
Below, the river is somnambulant mud;
moss lies in sand saucers; the hairy legs of roses gather glow
from the ground.

LEARNING A DEEPER COURTESY OF THE EYE

I

This is what you want.
You go into porcupine hills on a cold afternoon, down an aspen-ruffed
 path on Sam's land behind one low grass-knotted dune, then into real bush.
You will see deer.

Eros has nowhere to go but to become sorrow.
Piss marks on snow, flattenings,
creases where animals rolled, hoof-drag through drifts.
Exhaustion now as you walk toward the world's bright things.
Grass over snow, rose-hips clear and large in winter-killed thicket.
You will never make it all the way up to them.

II

The back fields are beautiful.
Take off your glove, coast
                    fingers through oatgrass tips.
Four deer fountain from the poplar circle where
last fall the dog and you lay in old fox beds, breathing.

It hurts to look at deer,
deer under their name.
The light from their bodies makes you ashamed
and you look down.

THE SOUL MUST LIVE IN THE INTELLIGIBLE WORLD

Summer and you dig in the ground
because a shovel conducts sadness into earth,
beckoning tears nitroglycerine down through itself into the black
seriousness of the world and home; down it penthos bucks,
                                        flaring at the shining tongue.
You dig in the ground because you want to see.
Today it's hot: last night thunder festooning over
gardens, touching its way,
earth dipping its head like a startled heifer and staring at it,
your raspberries yellowing from too much rain, two inches at sunset
                                        in half an hour, hail, theatrics,
earth fat, nimble today because of rain.
You dig in the ground because this starts the long path to virtue.
Potato tubers, Knights of Malta faces set as if they've taken a vow,
the frog skin, Godzilla skin of the leaves,
the potatoes are leaning into darkness, humming, idling pistons,
a pewter glow of intention ahead of them,
the potatoes are leaning into darkness
as they thickly dither into what they are.
You dig in the ground because you want to see.

Seeing receives a true, alto heaviness from work.
You sway, a black-tipped gold thing, then,
                    floating thing of no speech,
you sway downward and upward into the numen of cacti and wild rye.

EARLY JUNE, SANDHILLS

for S.

A path among deepest grass roots
bright as the dirty pearl of an old wound, heroic and far away.
The comedy of the height of trees winks at it.
The weight-shadowed path can be where it is and elation where it is.

You've planted some wheat; let it have a good time.
Here, there, this, now, the pert blades twaddle, and infinity.
The small wheat will lie like a sharp stone tool under the August moon
because what is wanted now is spectacles of silence and longing.
Breathy engine of the wheat,
patriotic, quake and drive.

DISCIPLINE OF SECRECY

Lie on your belly now, stare, pour into the golden
eye of the grain and be counted.
Engorge its face with your peering's heavy light.
The wheat gives you its plush inattention and
is therefore trustworthy.
It grew near your unborn face.
Let your weight bleed from you and fan into the wheat.
The wheat's moving rest will heft your desire and shape it
to itself.
Tell the wheat everything.
You have done nothing wrong and are naked.

You planted it by hand – someone to talk to.
The marrow of wheat is patience.
In its palm, the grain holds its one fixed heart,
nothing denser, nothing further away.
Ground is cold, sky lowered into it.
If you acted suddenly, not
watching yourself, the wheat's gold shadow, its
hiddenness, idea of beauty, would enter you
and make its home there.

Antlered wheat; like eros
it travels between the unknowable darkness
of sky and the unknowable darkness of earth.
The world is wide.
The wheat is trustworthy, sky thinking into soil.
In evening, thin pale flames over the fields, you see
this through aspens, the grain's ejaculatory flutter
under the aurora borealis.

SINGLEHEARTEDNESS

You are nailed to compunction.
Night deep in grass, the moon
between 3 and 4 a.m., lacrimae rerum.
You are listening.
Listening is straying in the snow-pintoed hills, sour March snow.
You find a black artichoke head, hand grenade forehead,
blistering, periscoping from frozen sand.
To find this is listening. Listening is waiting then digging out the whole
charred, rilled corpus and roping it to your back.
Body of the father, body of the god.
A railway tie shadow flaps against your buttocks, you must breathe for it.
This is weeping, this is listening.
You wear it, a steeple of bells, iron lung.
It smells of distance, smells of ancient water.
Your father's asphalt body flows in the bed of your body.
You wear it, standing over the sink, cloudy hump; eating, shaving,
you wear it.
Desire moves in it as tar in sun.
You confess to the muscular, reptile attention.
Its neck bulges, you know you must choose.

GOING INTO THE CLOUD

You must not think the drowsy, luminous weight, multi-breasted crops,
        loyal-to-itself grass, long conversations round a wine cup, will
rise, athletic, sure of itself, hefting from earth, heroing against light's
whispering thrust, wooed by the love of the One, nor
say all leaps against the decay of radiance, the flow downward which is
the debauchery of light, all things
leaping
to beach in the fixed, golden place
of a pure and distant absolute thinking, first place.

Desire nothing you can imagine.
You must sit on the thin hill grass.
Look south, open on your lap the heavy
                perfumed score of weeping.
Return to your place and begin again.
The path to take
is to find yourself forgotten.

INCUBATION

You sleep in wilderness, you sleep on your father's grave,
on dragon scales of hackled dirt, face down;
                    this is not the world.
There are flyways of cranes that smell palely of vegetation and mind
                              along dim southern rivers.
These are the light of what is, what makes a man
leave mother and father and, nude, set his cheek against its
                                             scented hurtling.
But you sleep on your father's grave, loam teat
in your mouth, milk like the light of cities
seen through an airplane window at night.
The vague, brilliant spawn will not draw.

Death is a straw bale hut in winter, his death
the notch of a high birch.
Enter the height and look out.
You sleep tingle-stiff with shadowy force, you sleep
                                        on your father's grave.

The measuring line has marked a lovely place for you, set your
          feet in a large room.

(A solar boat, a brain-calving grotto)
You want the food of his breath,
chewed, black, given into your mouth.
This will hold plans, a frail path into the world of particular things.

PARADISE OF THE CELLS

You lay down with unlooked-at things.
Poverty gave you this.
You came to these hills, dunes like shed antlers.

The land is deranged, someone pounding the ground
with his fists, howling.
Long, first grass a vase of tears, woven with hair,
set on the earth, hidden, low, the worth of the world.
You tried to be born in the animal's look.
You tried to live still among tracks in new snow.

Everything is odoured with infinity;
snow moves through high grass; everything is infinite.

SONG OF THE PROFOUND VIEW

You dug a cave in a south slope,
a black air hole stumps out –
you'll weep your way into the world.

Here, deny the Plato soul, angel soul, soul
          alive before birth in a brine of mathematics.
There is no visitation.
No golden lunges of mind, no staircase desire
                    ascends and descends in the heirloomed mind.
There is the sun in frozen corn, a pietá.

An eerie will-cry gropes through stubble smoke for cranes
eating dropped grain near the oxbow marsh; come, it says;
                              come now; do not worry.

SLEEPING ON THE LAND, SANDHILL HOLLOW

The glorified bodies of wheatgrass and brome flicker onto them;
nighthawks wing-bark down through bruised air.
You leave the house; the body has a question; the body
walks through angelizing grass.
Evening star out, Jupiter low to its left.
Slow, careful, fleshy hills hulk round ground nests,
eggs the colour of hot afternoons.
Private arrested rains of berries along ravines.
The blue of these fondles an ache into the chest.
Shadows in grass nudge the dark cells.
Here's the grove, attentive, white trunks, small water upliftings
in pale rinds, strumming.
Lay out the orange sleeping mat and bag.
What could the dead want of you?
This night has been lived in before, there are signs.
Faint spoor of consciousness.
Bulging poplar rhizomes below you.

There is a rest in things, level-bubble of ghostliness
in the moth-clotted dusk.
Poplars sway a wealthy, tended lack of purpose among themselves,
a sanctity beyond you.

For you, knowing comes through the body's wound.
The body whose weight is its loneliness for other bodies.
The moon rustles forth.
Knowing now is sleeping on the wild earth.
It is coming into the grasses,
the long grasses, crossing the border at night, thinking
how unclear the world is.
The grass is epic, mortal, it is blinding variety.
Sage leaf snags the end-thunders of light, wrestling in the
golden stresses.
The dark sniffs, circles, settles round.
In the Rapture all breaths will align,
but now the darkness is singlehearted and you are not.
It breathes wisely, beetling into you.

You dream the Polynesian breasts of a woman of hurtling density.
This is what's at stake, dogma, she rests then on the table, everyone looks.
You dreamt this for others; it could mean anything. She's the mass

of all looming, fish-like, pearly.
The moon is intense and of two minds in the sheeny dawn winds
you wake into in the rose-sharp fields.

SLEEPING ON THE LAND, ROOT CELLAR

August. Stars bulge against the world.
You lie down in the hole where you've stored potatoes,
their meaty antennae nod.
Above, a roof of straw bales.
On your lucky third night, you dream of passing
bears running in darkness-flickering grass.

You wish to understand the world? Be vanquished by it.
In one aspen yesterday, living like a spy, a
city of light.
Its depths, boulevards. Everywhere,
the aroma of thought. You have no rights in that city.

Desire thins the shape it rushes,
so the hole is your rest.
Under hawk-shouldered stars, crickets
and primrose, their distant, woody smell of sperm.

THE POVERTY DESIRE BELIEVES IN AND ARCHES TOWARD

You could drift into the unbreathable loneliness of other things.
You could float into the desert and building winter of the fawn.
Where would you live out there?
Indian summer now, light's vinegary dust, corn gardens rotting.
Let places of rest and hearing appear in the boiling, tearing-apart distance
where you can squat, wait,
a deer's vacant, glowing bed; a blow-out under juniper roots in the hills.

You want to know everything
and so lie down in the shallow pool of light
wildness has broken into oatgrass.
On the floor, iron scent of melted snow,
scat-crumble, the powers of grass.
Light breathes in green aspen.
Your knowledge is too clear.

DEER

Let them be ecstasied into us.
Let it hover from them, titanic, airy, body light, absent-minded
musics of muscle and eye, light
bottom-tipped with the first green inches of spring aspen mulch,
what their goldenness peers into us, moons, suns, el dorados
of motionlessness and glide, the white afternoons
of their bodies
drifted from them, nimbled into us massively and unmeant.
Let it find us as a mouth love-flesh bumbling in the great dark upon us,
their pollens of silence, their rest, fever halos, the blurred
far-light-in-the-forest of their difference,
brimming, the gathering antennae tremble round the wave-rilled edge of
the light of themselves, let it come.

DIAMOND WILLOW

You are the buck of thinking in history,
                                                    humped god
                                                                        abroad in the knotted garden of his momentum.
Spine-conducted silence, musky, self-leaving rush:
                                                                                        let me be one good thing.

Thronged silence, think of me.
You are remembering the king list of water
                                                under the earth.
Willow tree, force, sleep's liturgical stampede, a breathing.
You, wood, the plume of intention.
You, breathing, are the home lap.
My scars take the nipple in their mouths.

IN PARADISO

Technique is ourselves.

Snow in the dark trees, blizzard on the river.
The river's lope of amnesia, the river a forgetting that renews
and slenders itself whole.
Water black as what fills an eye rolling back into a head.
Obese river moults from alpine gestures, feathered
processions of the white horses of itself.
Sleep's its highest calling, through wild licorice, wild raspberry.
Now the moon over the buckskin earth,
now light, this light, an aural mirror, over glistering, dead grass.
Grouse have clawed into hard drift fold to live with their faeces.
You still do not understand the storm-bearing body
which is residence in other things, nor the good
lands beyond the eye.
Think of all you have not done.

Light smelling of lair, leafmould caught in the cleft of a hoof.
Guttural float of tonned light, impacted attention.
Moon over the river's blizzard, yarded hills, moon
over fox belly grooves in high drifts, over grouse
wedged in banks –

Desireless, an alkaline mask.
Polished curve of motion-smouldering stone
                                        that is the design of a voice,
full chord of itself in the mouth.
Herd bones, their constellations in winter-wet sand,
pluck at its orbit, the small touch
they're allowed, their love.
The moon swaying over the squat blood of the earth.
How to be here?
The souls of deer roil in their shoulder muscles,
                                        the weightlessness of aspens.
To think toward this, you must waft through marble.
The river loses itself forward across the plain.
Things sprout a called-back collar of gold,
                          the decay of something brighter.

GAZING AT THE WALL

The furnace has wavered out twice;
          afternoon moon in ice fog sags against earth.
Horse-calm hills and a mortal glimmer in air.
Ahead, in grass, beyond crouched snow clouds hulking through,
                              cliff edge of the century
and a black flicker of things that flow over it and are gone.

A brightness cakes the objects of the world,
grime of earlier seeings
and all we know.
The true world lives in a hovel further back.
Darker than chokecherry in winter, smart, out past hills,
                    rotting, past lynx trails, sunk down.
Light from us fattens us and loves us when we look at where objects are.
Time to learn to be homesick.

The air could kill us.
You walk through violet, embedded flames of cold.
You must recant the glamour of clarity.
The world, the world, you'd like to live inside a tree.

You have looked too hard for deer back in blow-outs and frozen
juniper, grasping for their marks on paths to place your
instep over them, this shining, have wanted to be let in, laid out grain
and waited, you have loved this light too much.

Take the dog, go through poplar deeper into hills,
the eye must learn an etiquette and exhaustion
                                                  before the distance of things.
Not a monk, watch the scoring deepen
as wind works a grass tip back and
forth across snow. This isn't prayer.
What's left is giving up entirely.
Everything falls short of theophany. It is itself.

HOW TO BE HERE?

I

Desire never leaves.

Looking at wolf willow bloom,
streaming through plushlands of scent toward the feeling
of its yellow,
self breaks up, flaring in stratosphere.
Looking undermines us.
The world and its shining can't hold our evaporating weight.
The world or what is there goes away
as we enter it, goes into halls of grass where torches of
darkness burn at noon.
Goes into light's lowest mind.
Leaving us, woo-floated from planet-like names and not quite
in things' shimmering gravity, alone in wide June air.
All-thumbs intensity that feels like virtue or music.

The Form quivers in the deer.
She doesn't see me; I'm lying barely above grass on a plank between fallen
poplars.

Hot day, slow wind; I lift on the cam of rhizomes.
The light behind her light is a shell she's just now born out of.
The Form is the doe's ease within herself.
I came from there.
If you dug with small tools into radiant belts round her shoulders
you'd come to a first settlement of the soul, stroke pottery bits, put
your tongue on old cinders and remember.
Tears will take you part of the way back but no further.

II

You wake, say, inside a large mosquito net,
you're away from yourself, older, near a desert perhaps,
air cool, dry, cloud of small sand, everything seems far
away, North African, night ancient, hard to read, you
look through the flap and see something bent toward a fire,
sparks low round it, stocky, sitting on its man-calves, force, tiptoed.
It is desire.
Yes, adding stick after stick, it seems,
managing in its naked hands
the reins of occurrence,
charioteering the will – horses of night.

You want to walk in the dark garden of the eye of the deer looking at you.
Want a male goldfinch to gallop you into the heart
                    of the distance which is the oddness of other things.
All would be well.
Desire never leaves.
Mercury's flower, a ghost-hurtling.

A mirror held before the spiritual wind
that blows from behind things,
bodying them out, filling them with the shapes and loves
of themselves.
You want that
and all else that shows in the bright surface polished by the lunge and
prowling of your desire.
You don't know what you are doing.

III

Desire tells me to sit in a tree.
I live alone, mentally clothed in the skins of wild things.
Desire sways ascent into me.
I look, I look: bull-necked hill, blue sweetgrass in hollows.
Knowing is a bowing, a covering of your face, before the world.
The tree's white tallness praises through me.
What receives the bow?
I am seduced by the shapeliness
                    of the failure of knowledge.
My name in religion is the anonymity of grass.
I practise dying.
Each day, the tutor, old man, eros, repeats the lesson,
              I wrinkle my brow, my tongue protrudes.
Outside the window one chokecherry in the bush,
in a thicket of gooseberries,
adds a weight and compression of darkness under the sun
                                        that is perfect.

RESTORATION

I want to be the knowledge that is one sleep in the sunward shoulder muscle
of the two-year-old doe coming out of hills and down to Moon Lake.
I will get there by seeing.
The whole body and virtue will rise up and form the look.
Seeing is the extreme courtesy that comes when desire is broken.
Desire will be broken and will continue with a bright limp.
We will move toward high bush cranberry and the smell of water.
I will be attentive, an oblique crescent near her spine, touched
by the light of her liquids. We will be going to Moon Lake,
the diamond willows,
old oxbow lake, reeds round it, the true river a ruin of water
in dust further on, the red century ending.
I will see my way into that place and into that body.
This will come only after I've been sitting in the long grass
eating loaves of shadow pressed up through the ground.
I will have been dreaming there of one day opening milky eyes and finding
myself sick, inside her body, high up, near the spine, poor, relieved.
Sometimes it happens: you lose everything
and wake in the strange room of what you want.

Except I won't be awake but asleep and full of gnosis.
In my ears, gold pulse of her footsteps.
We will go down the hill and enter the shadows of frost-burnt roses
and the shade of the smell of water in which reeds and elms are rotting,
October sunlight the shore of a country a small boat is just now pulling
away from.
I will smell her, light of one locked room in the mansion.
I will be in the muscle, a painting on the cave wall of her flesh.
I crane into the deer.
I am in the bright-dark cloud of knowing her
and could walk for days.
She is at the top of the hill and starting down
in early evening.

ACKNOWLEDGMENTS

I thank the Saskatchewan Arts Board and the Ontario Arts Council for financial assistance.

I am indebted to a number of friends for their encouragement and advice: Jan Zwicky, Anne Michaels, Don McKay, Seán Virgo, Dennis Lee. Knowing them has been one of the deep pleasures of the last few years.

I wish to thank St. Peter's College for its hospitality during the time in which this book was written.

The quotation that appears on page 18 is taken from *The Sayings of the Desert Fathers, The Alphabetical Collection,* translated by Benedicta Ward, SLG. The quotation on page 45 is a blending of lines from Psalms 16 and 31. The epigraph on page 56 is from George Grant's *Technology and Empire.*

*

Part of the feeling that attends returning to the world is the belief that restoration cannot occur – that and the impression of desire pushing past this conviction of impossibility. The deer still is at the valley lip, she is far away. The desire to see God, says Gregory of Nyssa, is the vision of God.

*

Some of these poems have previously appeared in *Fiddlehead*, *The Malahat Review*, and *Brick* magazine.